15th M

1

The Best

# The Bestiary

Sam Meekings

First published in 2008 by
Polygon, an imprint of Birlinn Limited
West Newington House
10 Newington Road
Edinburgh
EH9 1QS

*www.birlinn.co.uk*

ISBN10: 1 84697 046 6
ISBN13: 978 1 84697 046 7

*British Library Cataloguing-in-Publication Data*
A catalogue record for this book is available from the British Library.



Design and typeset by
Koinonia, Manchester
Printed and bound
by Bell & Bain Ltd, Glasgow

*for Leann and Sarah*

# Contents

## Water

## Air

# Water

# Frog

The initial incision sees it upturned
as if drunk and bloated, sizzling out gasps
like ghosts or wet farts: think of the thick lumps
and creases that gurgle up in old milk.

Next, the layer of mucous wrapped snug
beneath the pale sheaths of camouflage:
peel it back quickly, undress the hot mess
of tangled rubber bands from its slick embrace.

The textbook tells us that the frog lives
a double life: between sea and land, between
impossible distance and delayed arrival.

See, those jumpy chubby reels of twitching slime,
and this pip below the chin: the first voice
the universe heard, halved and inside-out.

# Snails

This is how it must have begun:
thunder, ghost tambourine skinning
the clouds and rattling out rain.

Never forget that this is the sea
stood up, practising levitation:
this time it paddles through you,

turning up puddles into laughs.
And on cue come the snails,
scattered down like bullet-shells

from a war everyone has forgotten.
Horned-heads darting out
from dappled backs, determined

to ooze inkily across the park,
to trail silver across the dark.
And yet still the rain stones them,

forgetting it unwrapped them
and handed them out like toffees
only seconds ago. That the rain

is forgetfulness made heavy,
full, fat, the snails will soon realise,
and clutch the soil instead,

just as a child clings to its mother's breast.
This is how it must have begun,
with longings and weather reports,

and even the pebble-sized snails
learning that everything
will have to wait for tomorrow.

# Depth

It seems like days before his eyes adjust
to the aubergine glow of the hugging dark,
feeling as though he is floating in phlegm:
bent knees pressed up to his twisted neck
in the roaring accordion of the whale's gut.

Jonah's world is composed of textures,
of shudders and damp echoes
tugging through his cold, aching body
and more fish frantically flapping in
every time the whale sings or swallows.

This is the depth to which we test ourselves,
he repeats. Soon his own wild shouts
join the booming chamber music.
His talking to God is similar to the tuning
of crackly CBs, late into lonely nights,

when solitary figures send cautious words
into the clumsy deep of rolling sound
and listen for something to return;
tentative voices testing the water,
each one prisoner of hearts and tongues.

# Crabs

With a fist of flint I pick back
the pale pack of crabs scaling
a husk of foamy driftwood,

which for them is an altar
to a malevolent god of shipwrecks
as rough as a cat's tongue.

I push to its hum – hunching
down to its hulking gravity
I begin to understand

the motion of yesterdays
struggling to catch us up.
When I reach out to touch it

my shadow is snapped off
by the waltzing breeze and carried,
flailing, dancing, out to sea.

# Night Tide

(Du Fu)


Crisp midnight clouds curdle in the waves,
torches slide across the shore; tightly curled
egrets nest on the sand-speckled banks.
Fish move like spirits, splashing between worlds.

# Turtles

No, it is not with the silent grace of stippled turtles
tipping wrinkled brows and batting back the water
that you take to the sea, but splashing up a flailing trail
of spray and elbows.

No, you never learnt to glide through it
like an old-fashioned flying machine, all glue and bone
lost in the continents of its dark. You know only splutters,
coughs, undercurrents.

Yes, this is where the dead go,
with turtles to the weightless empire of coral.
You stand at the shore and take the sky into your arms
as if it were a child.

# Fish Market

Nudged up between the dumpy autumn pears
and the Picasso man missing half his teeth,
a woman spreads out squirting mussels,
her stained shawl like a sprawling wreath.

She quiets hagglers with a tribal bark,
a puddle of shadows weighed in the slack
and turn of her hands, trawling slowly through
her army of haggard bargain blacks.

Only days ago I learnt the story
of a mussel that lived a thousand years,
pinched and stroked by the restless ocean;
lived slow and quiet as the sea's dark ear

closed tight against prayers; as the land learnt fire,
fists, how to speak in tongues, she was still,
until, with her long-learnt magic, she became
a girl. Her wing-like lungs took their fill

of soupy air, and she saw a fisherman
doubled by the dancing waves in the bay.
At first, she could not tell him from his twin,
until they severed and drifted away,

and by then it was love. Used to waiting,
she trailed his seaweed footprints for hours,
and while he wrestled with rain-sparked nets
she crept in to clean his empty house.

Soon after he caught her, sloping back home
across a ghostly shock of slowing sand,
they settled into their happy ending –
except for the ocean god's demand:

that she must sit crinkling in fire
for ninety-nine days to fully become flesh.
(We long for these kind of stories, where
the characters always choose love, and death.)

This creased and wheezing mussel woman
might be thinking the same thing now as me:
that she too came from flame and stories,
and that her years come sprawling from the sea.

And perhaps when she hunches off home,
she will remember the taste of the brine
licked from another's hungry lips,
or combing sand from her hair for the first time,

or seeing herself transformed in someone
else's eyes. The evening always brings
these hidden hints or possibilities
from the secret lives of the tiniest things.

# Herons

Perhaps we could spend a lifetime studying the ridges
of the water, the leaves and crisp packets swimming up
on the surface while something stirs under: our souls live,
like pike, trout, shimmering salmon, aching through the
    senses.

# Carp

Gasping an argument
clung from
this twitching arc:

I have a hook
fed through a carp.
Children could have named her,

monastic and shy
and celestial. I fold the hook
back through her throat

and glistening gill,
and she's off, scything
quickly like a burnt firefly

from a red-hot reflection.
Thrown back,
forgetfully sliding

through to the other side
of the mirror;
and if God is gone

I would only like
to give her this
and call it mine.

# Oysters

The floor is a fortune of shells
as we watch each other chewing
over a litter of broken sea-bones,

arched like painted crests,
pebble folds we have hollowed out.
There is a moment when neither

of us is here; rather we're being
spoken by the ocean's vocal cords,
akin to slowly flying-falling

or a first French kiss: slippery,
new, liquid, all flesh. This must be
how death tastes. Remember it.

# Prawns

Shoals of nipple-pink king prawns,
crisp with dewy crimson juice
and ribbed with garlic and slivers of ginger:
a thwarted alien invasion.

Peel off the wire rig of antennae bristling
at their rusty armour, that crackling husk
below the hunched-back battle helmet
of the olive-eyed troops.

The fizzling whirr, the grated lemon skin,
the knives and forks; at home in this world
of crashed-down spacecraft clatter,
in our battered and whistling wok.

# Seahorses

Perhaps once the soul was stuffed in
there was something left over: some
slither of light, some dancing burn
blistering into life with braying head;

perhaps these matchbox dragons stem
the birth of a little magic, moving the way
you quiver out of your clothes –
in a shuddering flood of question marks.

# Jellyfish

Like egg yolks gliding through slimy whites,
these jellyfish bobbing through pitchers of night:

dozens of curves and bubbles struggling for form
while knotted to billows of blossoming storm;

unravelling shocks of strand and spark,
ribboning parachutes, maps of the dark.

# River

Past the locked garden gate / it came carrying leaves.
We first learnt about death / from its rough drag and hum:
it spread like thick spilt ink / leaking into our games
and scoring through our maps / at Thames, Severn, Arun.

It might have been a chink / in the brittle landscape,
a typographic slip / turning us upside-down
so that we saw ourselves / in the shimmering people
trapped in the reflection / of a tiny drowning town.

From a window we'd watch / men draw fish from its curves
and children juggle nets / through its scales and ridges;
we bent like roots to it / and grew old while it drove
on to carve up cities / into blocks and bridges.

We first learnt about God / from its scattering of light:
from watching its shallows / where at the edge of day
distant figures gathered / to stand knee-deep, waiting
for it to wash their bones / clean, clean as a blank page.

# Eels

'from the shreds of skin thus detached come new ones'

– Pliny the Elder

1

The alchemy
            of racks and nets
hung
                        around his house;
   the light
                              juggled on the loch –
the night closes in on him.

            The water that was once
a miracle
            of guesswork and chance
is their dwelling place:
                        because
not even nothing
                  knows
                        this sharp darkness,
this blind
                  shudder through
surfaces made shaky
                        by the haunting of his
deep
      and cloying breath.

The trap
                        of newspaper he carries
to wrap them in

          bears testament

                   to events

more than a decade

                dulled and faded;

      it seems even our local histories

cannot

        sustain

           this hungry dark,

bitten back by black backs

          and pale bellies.


And in the dance

           that his hands give –

and that this flesh

         on flesh

            on flesh is –

he is quick with it,

          struggling

            slivering

up his thick forearm:

               there is no

        such thing

as stillness.


2


        Splayed out

           on market stalls

spotted

      across the London that Dickens drew up:

potted, jellied, battered, broiled, fried;

                but not in this city

that has been built

from the sky down,
and where the trembles
of snaking underground trains
ripple
across our windows.

And if
within this seismic network
of veins
that cross
and re-cross
there is an undercurrent
that moves us
closer
to one another
it might be like these
reels of skin
moving towards
a sacred destination,
knowing nothing
of coordinates, of direction,
only drawing
knots
on the floor
of the still water.


3


The meadow grass
is alive
with silver,
in shocks the stems bend toward the stew,
with listless sparks.

           In kisses

and caresses

                    the world is

        moved

            and is mapped

      on this dry stretch

            between two spaces

of which we know nothing,

             between

then and now. Taste

        this dripping

            rich fillet

spluttered from the pan

                glistening with

        gliding slime

and think of this

        short flight:

  the meadow grass

        is alive.


4


        What Aristotle

   called

     'the entrails of the earth',

are a tangle of insomniac

            muscle:

everything is seen

        by the blind senses,

everything is seen

   in reflection.

They are

                           an erratic spine
    sending shipping forecasts
across a giant body,
                 moving like an uncracked code
                        or a wriggling
alphabet traced beneath the skin.


                     These nooks and crannies
are their hiding places:
              the spear
               inches above them,
clammy, closer,
             such
fierce machines
             such
wild midnight feasts.


5


                The boat he left
abandoned, a wreck
              tethered to a stump
of cut oak.
          The water
is restless
       without the blinking
               of his billowing
flashlight
       slurring up the lake,
                looking for his
strange children:
         those tumbling

                              bundles of liquorice
long gone
              for the ocean –
                              transformed.


                        And there the trail ends:
       the impossible
                        migrations
                              of the heart
are spurred, stinging instinct.


                        In a coal parlour
chilblains and calluses
                  are rubbed over smoke;
                        a huddling crowd
waiting
       for the scrape
                  of the door,
for transparent ancestral ghosts
                  to throw down their bags and settle
after so long by the fire;

                              waiting
              for the bite to take
and twitch
       the line back
                  back
                        into life.

# Arctic

Brute hunches, pillars of simmered-down filament
hulk through the six o'clock news.

These must be the limits of our grace –
the known and unknown, a fragile beauty

like this year's crop of calves baptised with bristly tongues.
These our broken psalms: slowing through time-zones,

whole continents dislodged into swarms of cataracts,
reams of light made thick through stubborn strength.

This is the farthest we can go before we return,
turning across the edge of atlases, the newsreel stuck

on those flayed bones floating round the compass,
herds of white elephants tentatively testing the currents.

## Travels in a City of Rooks

A row of rooks hangs like shadows on the parapets.
An old man guts a whale with an army penknife;
others lie tangled in hammocks like fish in nets.

Ragged cats stare lovingly at milk-fat mice,
and from the fall of fag ash futures are read:
I could remain a stranger here all my life.

# Harbour Music

Riddled with divots of silver where the moonlight dips
in between the planks, the boat seesaws on their shoulders.

It is spackled with spots of tar that stick to sweaty hands;
they tumble it down as if it were a kind of birth –

a tug-of-war with the water, the hush and knuckle
tussle till it crackles forward from the gravel.

The sea calls them in with a muffle of splashes,
and already I can guess where all this will end –

standing alone on the edge of this slipping bank,
listening to that slim wooden ribcage ripple away.

Soon the distant thumb-smudge hunch of rock
turns orange, and I watch the island

blister into life, tugging the sky from the sway.
By now the boat has become a bobbing comma.

A muzzle of gulls graze nets tied from thick cobwebs,
nets set by to plough the waves for bronze.

My eyes sweep back to the half-inch island
hogging the horizon-line, hovering above the boat,

the twist and shift of perspective it demands,
the wishes it pulls toward disaster. Waves jostle,

drag it farther. The gulls blur back into focus,
casually scraping the surface and turning up tails –

and because the impossible edge is calling
all sense from sight, I'm left staring at a panting fish

plucked up by eager beaks and spun into the clouds.
By now walkers stalk the shore, blocking the watch,

plastic bags lapping their feet, foam teasing footprints.
The island centres the sea like a corkscrew –

somewhere in its midst the boat has disappeared
deeper into the mist-thick distance, fast-forward.

I set back home, still watching as I go: sharp blues
where they might now be, tipping over into the brink

of possibility. Might all our movements shrink
to this – subtle, swallowed, indistinct? Our lives drift

between the push and shove, the sink and swim –
I will return tonight to help them haul back in.

# Air

# Dissection

First day I learnt how to cleave the earth in two
and stretch in up to the elbow to pull out
its offal, hot and sleek with wrinkled memories.

It was midnight before I found yours,
as tight as a tiny glistening mouth.
I prized it open with fingers and fists –

all the things we never said came hissing out
and made me old in a second. They were shadows
that were once your scrapbook hopes.

They were everything we might have done.
Second day I learnt how to crave you
like a plague of tics gluey at my skin.

Third day I learnt how to stitch the earth back up
at the frayed edges, how to conjure bones,
and that the way to kill a thing is with words.

# A Solitary Goose

(Du Fu)


Speckled, searching, soaring through the lonely
wind: a milk-white goose, crying as it flies.
It is a fluttering shadow come loose,
lost in tangles of broken cloud and sky.
It howls like a banshee, beating its wings
like a hopeless angel, a pale stray.
Wild ducks holler back, begin to sing:
the calls mingle and mix, then drift away.

# Sewing Machine

My mother always at an almost heirloom,
its whirring work that seemed to link everything –

a graveyard of roof-tiles held tight
night after night the year the gales claimed every other

or Friday night closing time at the local A & E
conjuring glass from rivers of skin –

with the patience of a seismograph needle
singing to an empty room;

making sense of a chaos of little holes,
our lives between the seams.

Nametags scurried down the back of our necks,
cuffs, backpacks; patches pulled us into our fittings.

We lined up in silence, as if it were an altar
at which were given countless lives,

where the tresses and tears of our eyelids, fingers, lips
were all stitched to the hem of the sky.

# Ellipsis

When you found that trio of hedgehogs bumbling about
between the dustbins and next door's fence,
freezing to the spot as soon as the torch caught them,
in their panzer formation I saw a perfect ellipsis.

They didn't return the next day, or the one after that,
despite us leaving titbits trailed across the lawn.
Perhaps they have slowly slunk beyond the woods
towards the places, dates and names we forget.

And because this drive is unstoppable, stuttering back
like cliff-side villages that have been slipping,
year upon year, further in, we surrender land
to the distances travelled after memory, giving over

to the things that lead us stumbling from ourselves.
A perfect ellipsis; like the hedgehogs, the few freckles
dotting your arm, or the three lopped-down oak stumps
where the edge of the park thumbs the school fence.

The hedgehogs must have sense of the parts of our lives
we leave in other places. We still put scraps at the edge
of the garden, right there, where our wandering thoughts,
like little kids with sparklers, shred through shadows.

# Hearing Things

A sound is this: a knot of rope fed through blistered fingers,
tracing a way across the minotaur country
of the coiling canals that make up the winding inner ear.

It is a handful of frantic atoms that move like wind chimes
in abandoned temples, keening with the wind:
whirling echoes left to linger in the lonely crags of cliffs.

The outer ear is a rung of discarded peel, a mess of folded flesh
worn like paper flowers on faded lapels.
It is this: being lost in the snaking alleys of a forgotten town

on the verge of speech, or a whole country inside a seashell,
where a hurricane butterfly might alight
on a skull mistaken for the mossy blossom of a stone.

# Fistful of Rabbits

His hands are too creased for the sleight
that draws your attention away from the trick.

He slithers in his suit, which wears him as a prayer
against the wind. It used to hug him tighter.

It's on the tip of his tongue, the way to turn it back.
What if our secrets crept out, hungry and all-teeth

each night to reclaim flesh? He wears his eyelids
like the ruined spire of a church seen only in ghost films.

Sometimes when the town pulls itself in
like an old blanket, and the night is summoned up

from the wild borders of splintered bed posts,
he wrings his hands, closes eyes, and is young again:

a burning deck of cards, three stray rabbits,
something halved, disappeared.

# Nettles

Between our village and the next, past the ruins
of a rust-sleeved spitfire, beyond a cauldron of stones,

sit a shroud of nettles, almost beckoning. Hidden among
a quiet committee of weeds, a trap for pockmarked hands.

Become a child again: dare them, taunt, skip, fall.
Loners in overgrown raincoats stride through their thick,

scarred from the surroundings; and then those looking
for nettle soup, for the impossible origin of things.

It is not here, on this overgrown path split
between the needles and the tough brows of dock

forever in their wake. Know this: the earth should not
be touched raw – it burns, bites, mourns your touch.

Tugging up these weeds is a fragile operation,
fumbling at spitting plug-sockets embedded in the mud.

Speckled hands can later be held up as trophies,
or scratched till sore and hidden in pockets.

Behind these prickly leaves stand grubby gravestones
whose letters have been scrubbed clean and bare

as have the relics of our past lives: stinging games
of kiss-chase, bodies painted with rashes and blushes.

# Mouse

It was snuggled small in your desk drawer,
smooth and clammy, the colour of washed coral:
that foetal mouse. You froze when you saw it,
coil of flesh clumsily bound in downy clingfilm.

Your period disappeared for months, as if something
so undone might undo you too; as if this trick,
this hidden crust of half-formed knotted fist,
was enough to shake off all beginnings.

Everything about it seemed shrunken;
a tight and frightening caricature of stillness,
a leering mouse with its wound of a mouth
as though carved in a nub of butter.

You knew even then that there are no guides
for this kind of half-done death, turning up
only in corners of dreams, old drawers, or black sermons:
that stunted petal of almost ear, that snub inch of tail.

# Hare

Turfed up from the tethers of tumbling plots,
a loose fit of jiggling legs wriggling in a sack of skin.

I watch it from the window, an arrow shot through
a thicket of weeds and gangly creepers.

I could not tame this restlessness with hutches
or burrows, nor tempt it in with coos or clicks.

It is a mess of tangled hunting gloves, something
that does not know belonging, does not need names.

I shuffle closer and scare it from the garden – gone
riddling the breaks of bracken, tall grass, barley;

like a blind Midas feeling a way home,
unaware of how his weathered hands are turning the maize.

# Bees

King Ethelbert of Kent met the missionaries
in the open air, fearing their incantations
would raise bones from his whispering fields.

Instead their honey breath drew up stones
into his fledgling cities, like bees breaking ranks
around a perfect slab of dribbling comb.

Men watched them weave a hive of ghosts
from the charred tang of thick shadows.
Pale palms and bleach-rim haloes poured

from the stained-glass, stretching the light
past eyes staring up, amazed at the vast sky
being compiled, brick by brick above them.

# Tortoise

Imagine, if you will, a crumpled queen of clubs
slowly eaten by algae: a bulging stone missing
from the cast of the zodiac. Each movement
it makes is a lifetime; these creased lines
of rough linen could be a beggar's old shoe.

The earth owns such strange toys,
like this wrinkled sage cut from clockwork.
Its slowness is a kind of grace,
an ocean's rusty joke; it sees life
as only the snapping of little jaws.

Is it true that everything begins in dreams,
all strange possibilities, like this addition to
god's black armoury, this green eagle-skull
stuffed in a junkyard husk? The tortoise is born
from the peculiar bestiary of the imagination.

And imagine again if it were possible to nose
this engine over and spill its slowness
over the kitchen floor; what would it do
on its back in an upside-down world
where whole seconds seem centuries?

# Nativity

A tea-towel gallery of battered lambs,
with missing eyes and dirty dog-tugged hooves,
clutched tightly under arms. A cardboard star
shakes above the wonky tinsel haloes.

The wise men are a shower of purple,
floating on and off like dislodged icebergs
into shadow. Others mull, banging drums
or latching onto arms to stay awake.

A curved crook points to a shabby manger
where a huddle of shrouds are rustling
under the weight of a half-remembered line.
It finally splutters into life, takes flight.

Mary holds her hands over her lumpy bump,
loudly faking surprise and gratitude
at the useless plastic gifts. Joseph searches
for his mum in the dark and muffled seats.

He is uneasy around the blonde doll.
Teachers crouching in the dim-lit wings
nudge and whisper the forgotten script.
Everyone stares up at the fizzing rain

of glass and light as a bulb shatters
and spills down a benediction of sparks,
all except the girl with paper wings
who believes she is an angel.

# Swan

If I close my eyes
I am a swan in the ruins
hunting for breadcrumbs
back where our fingers first touched
and the plumed birds strode like kings.

# Calves

Slow among the tall grass,
this year's gift of calves hobbling
hopefully; we see them each
morning munching at the scenery.

So brittle, so fragile those first steps.
The whole earth holds it breath
in our breath as they tilt forward
like frightened dolls on stilts.

Your clammy hand fed into mine,
and with each faltering step, with
each pale misshapen calf wobbling,
clutched tighter. Soon the mother too

comes nudging, holding her swaying gait
like a foreign dictator in a country
unutterably cluttered with the past.
You willed each one of them up

through the squeeze of your hand
tight in mine. I don't know how long
we watched for. I don't know whether
they were messages for our lost chances.

They told us to give in to stumbling,
give ourselves over to the impossible
again. Your ring dug into my palm
and we left them to the fields.

When we turned to go they buckled
and fell, the first fall, the hardest.
We left them bowing to the earth,
knees pressing down to push back up.

That night they came slowly lolling
into our bedroom, chewing the curtains
and lowing at the phone. Or perhaps
it was only how our hopes took shape.

Hold on tighter and the earth submits
to a memory of calves: it needs
these tiny miracles, these quiet longings
to which our bodies are bound.

# The Butcher

By this rubbed-pink pig's trotter
he contemplates the point from which
the universe expands exponentially,
between two outsized ogre's hands.

He pauses between the hanging racks
to listen for the buzz of flies through
his cinema of the invisible. Wipes
podgy paws on folds of sticky apron

and practises walking backwards.
He scalps and slices thick cuts
as if he is cauterising the stale air,
then ties them tight with paper and string.

His heartbeat bubbles in the stock
boiled from leftover bones. What god
imagined him, moving through time,
always washing his greying hands?

Chicken heads, pig livers, lamb; world
shrinks tight to a point where it forms
at his throat. Hieroglyphics fizzle
on the cold-room walls, waiting by

the stretched skin of weightless lives.
He sharpens knives, cleavers, clenches
his fists to warm his fingers. He bites
his tongue to stop it from muttering.

He cleans this floating meat-hook
in the ice breath of the dark;
by morning it will have caught another
cold carcass, another shivering dream.

# School of Rushes

(Dante, *Purgatorio*: Canto I, 112–136)


Starting down the slanting path I watched his gaze,
following, placing my feet in his footprints,
into where the valley cleaved the night from day.

The passing vale seemed as if it had been kissed
by a breeze from some distant sea; his cautious frown
seemed blessed by the soaring spectral sheet of mist.

We wandered like those lost, afraid to make a sound,
until he stopped in the glimmer of the shade;
then he bent down till his hands grazed the ground

and I knelt beside him in that silent place,
so close that I could feel his ghostly breath
as with his wrinkled hands he washed my ashen face.

We walked on, until we reached the shadowy edge
of the dark shore, where the tall rushes grew,
and he tore one up and bound it tightly round my chest.

My face still dressed with the light tears of dew
as a new rush sprung from where he'd torn one up –
as if a single touch could make the whole earth new.

# Describing Angels to the Blind

Acronychal mosquitoes lolloping
like strange machines patented from erotic daydreams.
They whistle in B flat, rattling the cutlery;
their breath is fingers in the plug socket.

Their wings are lopsided like dislocated shoulder blades
or the feel of another tongue sucked into your mouth.
They are the things that as a child you were not allowed to
    touch;
their voices table-salt on paper-cuts.

They carry the reek of moths sautéed in the lampshade,
of dredged-up reservoirs and spoiled meat;
their faces are the pumice stone you take to your feet.

Their language is a live catfish wriggling through your hands
or a tic or twitch you can't control,
their half-human faces a fit of giggles at a funeral.

# Mackerel Sky

### 1

After a storm, the gorse rises like ghosts
made flesh again by reels of rain and hail –
rearing up around parks, matting footpaths,
throwing shadows over slow-crossing snails.

The same could be said of our smallest hopes,
which creep back into the hollows of our hearts
and patiently take up their brittle stitch-work
which the rain and wind have ripped apart.

### 2

There is a dog, kept by a restless god
of death, who slowly chews and eats the moon.
And how does it taste? Of sleep and honey,
of shark-fin and cedar-wood and cashew.

And while his master welcomes lost travellers
and offers that they drink with him of death,
he snarls and barks at the pink-tinged distance
as if the broken clouds were a spreading net.

### 3

Marco Polo wrote of spirit voices
calling men away from fading tracks.
We spend out winding travels learning
that once you leave you can't come back.

Or else our lives are spent returning
to where we believe they must begin.
Spirit voices are like the worst hangovers,
leaving you lost in your own loose-fitting skin.


4

It was a surprise, after I had died,
to find that I wasn't where I belonged.
So, pushing through the creeping weeds and algae,
I came back from the skanky garden pond.

I ran inside while the sky turned to rags.
I spend this new life spying through the cracks
in the doors and walls, watching you carry on
and wondering how to tell you I've come back.


5

Remember: bus stops between cities,
watching shreds of circus cirrus change shape:
just like our friends dropping everything
to effect a carefully staged escape.

How quickly it came, the colours draining.
Our bodies meeting, crouched together,
our heads gently wetted where shreds of rain
crept through our worn and tattered umbrella.

6

There are winter spells our ancestors knew –
how to draw warmth from dull stretches of snow,
how to conjure the thread of gentle voices
from scattered knuckles of thatch, slate, stone.

The garden is a slush crushed beneath boots,
a blank slate, and from somewhere near
strays yelp and call in urgent, broken verbs,
not knowing that the winter has grown ears.


7

If you had any doubts, you boxed them up
when you took my hand and drew me in.
I love you like a muddle of dark hands
love a bonfire in a broken dustbin.

It seems so strange to let this love have rein:
above us, so close I can define the pull
of each feather, birds are driving south,
soaring and drawing in the clouds as they fall.


8

As she loved him, she pulled her fish body
from the wet dredges of the dark river,
and shed her skin and fins and gills and scales.
He watched her naked flesh twitch and shiver.

Because we go as far as is required.
And that is why the peeled sky also bleeds:
watch, rows of close-skinned cloud skimming through
the bowed and blessed heads of bending trees.

# Bat

A flap of tattered black leather
pulled taut over a rung of knuckle;

a matted head of a broken broom,
or the slick fuzz that dams the drain;

a blind spot of coal at the heart
of your pupil, staring out death;

fleshy thick folds of dark labia;
the chewed and ragged shame of a stray;

or the anatomy of a bruise: quivering,
vengeful, hidden from the world.

# Albatross

Coleridge
asleep.

The dewy skeletal beak of his gaunt pipe
jostling against the inkpots on his desk

points at
the window.

Outside the flying dinosaur is gliding
through a concerto of fog, all feather and mouth:

the albatross
is dreaming up Coleridge

who is dreaming that from his hunched shoulders
bristly bones are beginning to grow.

# Monsoon

The old woman with the wicker brush sweeping spiderwebs
from the shorter gawky trees
reminds me of how the wind begins,
as she unpicks the tricks of the tangled weave.

I think of the way lazy sows skim snouts
across the surface of a thirsty trough;
plump cocoons fidgeting, starting to flap;
something rustling through rusty haystacks.

The old woman has slipped between the trees;
the spiders are saving up their strength.
In the attic her dusty ballet shoes attest
to a world born from the slightest of dreams –
as the wind wakes the house with its calls
and dawn creeps in, peeling night from the walls.

# Dragonfly

You might as well try to tame that lock of brambles
with a child's podgy hands, or tie the sky
into knots and ribbons, as attempt to catch
that purring dragonfly between thumb and forefinger.

A slim treat noisily nosing in from the window,
its giddy reel inseparable from the chaos it sweeps over:
the guidebooks and street maps of invented places,
a book of days, the plans you were not meant to keep.

You might as well try to dream yourself a chrysalis
as entrap it under an empty glass. Wait.
Where will it spill from next? A flapping in the margin,
an itch in your hair; here, this small full stop.

# Listening to the Language of the Birds

(Li Bai)


The sky creeps along the city walls: clouds and crows
alight from branches, telephone poles, narrow lanes.
In a canal-side flat a girl is knitting clothes
from fog, mist, drizzle. She hears the birds' black refrain
and waits: her hands are stopped trains, endlessly delayed;
her hope is this empty room; her tears are the rain.

# Compass

God-tongued iron dart brought down by monks,
a fortune-telling floating lodestone, turned to oceans:
a pocket full of places. I thumb this relic of direction

and remember the story of lost sailors at last
returning home and tasting the earth in thick and literal
mouthfuls. What is it we crave from the mind's atlas

that drives us through such dark stretches of desire?
We cross and stitch our bodies into maps of faith.
This shiver of sharp rain, this crease in my hands,

all south/north. A tightrope-walker's trajectory,
scored between the parallel edges of a flat earth,
leading us on – to an overgrown pathway, a ruin of stars, sky.

# Geese

Among this clutter of crammed-tight bulging boxes
on a bare wooden floor, from this rigid high window,

I think I can imagine how the drifting geese might see,
halting midway through migration to glance down:

from this distance everything seems foreign or forgotten.
From here they might, like me, see this lost couple

slowing past the shop fronts of the empty street, navigating
the dustbins and bus stops. Further on, a hole in time

where an old woman sits among wonky picture frames
that haunt her sprawling stall. The couple stop, speak with
    hands

and pet the lanky mongrel emperor enthroned
by flaking chests of drawers and brown, faded globes.

This is what the geese would see if they dipped down and
    landed here,
appearing with the morning between my half-open curtains:

the old woman among empty birdcages, music boxes,
fold-up tables overflowing on the scrum-locked cobblestones.

And they might make out the remnants of a movement
that can never end, clues among the junk of other voyages:

the map the couple shake and turn until it reshapes the street,
the torn corners of their travelogue, and back at the stall

the souvenir plates, the way the woman talks to her dog,
the reason everywhere else is boarded up. Above,

a paper airplane that flutters near loops and nosedives down,
cutting through to the present. I have never been this far from
    home.


2

My grandmother's gaggle acted like an army of guard dogs,
flaring up around water and chasing scared strangers

in a blizzard of cackles and lunges. My brother and I planned
to fatten them up with brick-thick crusts of hardened bread,

but backed away when their gossipy waddles threatened to
    turn
into a whirl of stinging beaks. Instead we hid in mushroom
    sheds

or sat on the skeletal shell of a tractor to watch them harass
    others
from afar. As far as we knew they never went anywhere,

even when the skinny fingers of winter teased a trail of ice
across the sloping barns of their farm, preferring to huddle

inside where the hay bales had once been piled. Looking back
it might be easy to attribute this to clipped wings, the cut
    strings

of soaring hopes. But in their blank chatter and endless
circling of the same plots I see them now as lost amnesiacs,

patiently trying to forge meaning from the steady spray of the
river,
to tempt memory from the dark scent of feather-like wild
flowers.

Staring out from the mushroom sheds in daylong games
of hide-and-seek, I never considered that their jerking
movements

were a way of searching for a forgotten, impossible purpose.
I feel a bitter kinship with those restless birds. Only now,

among the restless paraphernalia of the muddled past
do I see the strange intimacy between us, young boys

wearing our coats as capes, and those raucous, barking geese,
both hopelessly trying to learn how to fly.

---

3

The window becomes a lesson in skylines: a neglected history
of rooftops, one fit for drifting geese. It creaks open.

How might such a history begin? With the speckled scales
of slanting slates on grey tenements, and the stubby thumbs

of chimneys blossoming like the first fat crops of a stone
harvest.
Puddles of sliding skylights blink between them.

Thin rigs and boards of black scaffolding are draped like
        netting
over the buildings, and tips of trees nestling like extras

in the dregs of a loft scene lean toward the distant reach
where colours mingle with staccato gasps of cloud.

Nothing lies beneath the drain ridge collecting rain;
the world of walking is one the landscape has forgotten.

Above, the three bent 'M's stretched on the fault-line
might be geese driving toward the edge,

the point the eye and mind cannot yet formulate: beyond
perspective. These are geese that do not need to be seen

to exist, flying like flaying work shirts escaped
from the washing line; these are geese to believe in,

slim fictions like our own invisible migrations; geese
that, like us high in attics, barely flutter up a footnote

in history books. I pull the curtains on this mess
of oil and eaves and measure out another glass of wine.

The gulls push out from the roof like cautious schooners,
rippling across the palest folds of the fraying sky.


4


Snow geese must believe in karma: eternally returning
to where their dappled eggs lie like unwound bandages,

ready to begin again. Even the goslings, blotted with blue,
start by mimicking the largest of the flock, tentatively mapping

the traps and marks of the nesting ground. Among the
     terraces
those jagged V formations splay the billows of cloud

across the sky, their rusty grey bellies shifting above us,
already disappearing into the past. The sun melts

like an orange ice-lolly onto the doughy folds of far-off hills,
and I wonder what has become of the landscape of my
     childhood:

the knotted wood of my first bed; the weeds snuggling up
among the paving stones; my electric-blue bike, studded

with stabilisers; the broken stitching of grass-stained trousers;
my grandmother's geese conquering the corners of the farm.

I open the window and try to watch the shocks of ivory
beginning to blur at the horizon-line, the hoot and howl

trawling toward some distant scatter of marsh, fading from
     sight.
Across the street a lone window throws a sharp light

into the sky as two bodies move together between its jaws,
move with the fragile grace of flight, as if they might

cease to exist should their slow embrace be broken. Perhaps
they too know that all stories must end with a beginning,

flowing flesh grazing flowing flesh on the fold-out bed. Or else
like the geese they have guessed that there are a thousand ways

of crossing the earth, and a thousand ways of returning,
slowly drawing sounds from one another's throats.

# The Anatomy Lesson

The Waaggebouw, Amsterdam, January 1632

This is not death. Here, behind these origami eyelids
are fireflies swimming in thickened cream. Look –
knowledge means seeing things backwards, as if
unravelling codes from knots in sailors' matted nets.

The jaw locks on impossible corridors. The throat
can be used as a periscope hoisting longing
from the dark. The heart, cage within a cage,
is chamber music for the homeless and forgotten –

it can only rest, you'll understand, when placed,
as we will see, in the palm of a hand. Follow
these vascular rigs that lead like schools of herring
hurrying between the borders of understanding –

though, of course, gentlemen, just give us time.
The body, you will see, does not die. These finely sliced
fingerprints could be rivers of gauze, gradient surveys,
or the fluttering wings of prehistoric moths.

This stub of tongue is a rope thrown out for lifeboats.
We must see the logic in this or fall. Hold this hand
while I make the first incision – here, let it lead where
you will walk. Even the stillest of bodies will talk.